THE SYSTEM
OF SEX

THE SYSTEM OF SEX: SPIRITUAL DIVORCE

AND WHY YOU NEED ONE

LUDIE BENEL-PONCE, M.A.

DISCLAIMER

The material in this book is provided for spiritual, educational and inspirational purposes only. The author does not offer medical, psychological, or legal advice. It is not intended as a substitute for professional medical, psychological, or pastoral counseling. Readers are encouraged to seek qualified professional advice for individual concerns.

DEDICATION

First and foremost, all glory and honor belong to my Lord and Savior, Jesus Christ. Every revelation in this book comes from His Spirit, and every page is marked by His mercy. He is the One who healed me, freed me, and taught me the truth about covenant, and the One who empowered me to write this for you.

To my husband, Luis,

Babe, thank you for being a steady witness of God's love to me. Thank you for pushing me toward obedience when it would have been easier to shrink back. Thank you for covering me, praying for me, and reminding me who I am in God when the assignment felt heavy.

Your love strengthens me. Your faith anchors me. Your leadership sharpens me. Thank you for loving me with a love that reflects Christ; deep, patient, and undeserved. This book exists because God is faithful, and because you never let me forget it.

I love you so much!

And to the one who feels bound...

To the one carrying silent memories, hidden pain, or a connection you can't seem to break.

This book is for you.

I wrote this with you in my heart.

Not to expose you, but to free you.

Not to shame you, but to remind you who you are.

Not to reopen wounds, but to show you the God who still heals them.

I pray these pages bring clarity where there has been confusion, peace where there has been torment, and restoration where there has been loss.

You are not alone. You are not forgotten. And you are not beyond freedom.

May this be the beginning of your release, your restoration, and your return to wholeness.

God is faithful, and your story isn't over.

TABLE OF CONTENTS

INTRODUCTION

Culture has a lot to say about sex. If we only consider what we receive from television, social media, and even so-called "experts," we will be deceived, and unknowingly diminish the true weight and nature of sex. Despite what we are being led to believe, sex is not simply fun or for pleasure; something to be done whenever or with whomever. Sex is a system.

Sex is deeper than pleasure, more than just connection, and more profound than procreation. It is a system created by God, to unite two individuals into one entity, while also serving as a maintenance system for this convergence.

Sex is not purely a physical act; it is also emotional, biological, and deeply spiritual. Sex does not end once we complete the physical act and get up from the bed;

it continues in our physical body, our emotions, and our soul.

Unfortunately, many of us have had sex outside of marriage and are now realizing the depth, influence, and effect sex has had on our lives. A breakup is not sufficient to break the bonds and bring freedom from the emotional ties that were formed. Moving hundreds of miles away does not make the person disappear from our hearts, our minds, or our souls. Some of us have been praying for a spouse, not realizing that there is one already laying claim to us in the spirit. We are being blocked by the unseen.

If you feel bound by a past sexual relationship or are struggling with pornography and/or masturbation, there is hope. As we study God's system of sex, not only do we look at the spiritual ramifications of premarital sex, but we also evaluate the biological effects of sex and the power of its impact on our lives.

This book will not only arm you with information, but most importantly, it contains powerful chain-breaking, deliverance-inducing prayers for freedom from soul ties, pornography, and masturbation. For many of us, this book is an answer to prayer, not only for ourselves, but even for our future generations.

PART I
SOUL TIES

Have you ever wondered why you cannot get that person out of your head after having sex with them? No matter what you do. It is as if they have become a part of you. You do not even want to be around them, but your emotions, body, and mind seem not to have received the memo.

You try to move on, and the second someone new steps into your life, the ex starts calling, texting, DM-ing, and even showing up. You are not even in a relationship, and yet, it feels like they can smell that there is someone new in your life. If you did not think it sounded crazy, you would think they are stalking you. It is as if they have a sense that you are moving on, and they must pull you back. Like there is a spiritual reporting system that you are not aware of.

As you read further, you will discover that you are, in fact, picking up on something. It is called a soul tie. This is something I have experienced firsthand, and it was only through revelation that God provided me with the solution to this phenomenon.

A soul tie is deeper than just lingering thoughts, feelings, or difficulty letting go of a relationship. It can also manifest through habits and thought patterns that were once completely foreign but now feel alarmingly natural. Suddenly, you are battling struggles you have never known before all because of intimacy with that particular person. It becomes a grip you cannot seem to break free from.

While the term "soul tie" is not directly in the Bible, we do find in multiple places where we are told a man and a woman become "one flesh."

Genesis 2:24 24 (NKJV) Therefore a man shall leave his father and mother and be[k] joined to his wife, and they shall become one flesh.

Additionally, a soul tie can go beyond a sexual relationship. Scripture provides us with a visual of a non-sexual soul tie through the relationship of David and Jonathan.

1 Samuel 18:1 (NKJ "Now when he had finished speaking to Saul, the [a]soul of Jonathan was knit to the soul of David, and Jonathan loved him as his own soul."

Science also does not submit to the term "soul tie." Instead, they use terms like "attachment theory, trauma bonding, codependency, emotional imprinting and memory."[1] According to Psypost.org, all these terms are used in the Psychology world to describe what Christians identify as a soul tie.

In a recent article on Brides.com, psychotherapist, Chamin Ajjan, stated this about soul ties: *"It's not just a fleeting connection—it's a bond that leaves an imprint on your well-being, your growth, and how you see yourself and the world—for better or worse,"* says Ajjan. *"These connections go beyond surface-level*

---

[1] Dolan, Eric W. *"Soul Ties: Exploring a Popular Belief in Deep Emotional Bonds."* **PsyPost**, 22 Mar. 2025, https://www.psypost.org/soul-ties-exploring-a-popular-belief-in-deep-emotional-bonds/.

interactions and shape you in ways that are hard to ignore."[2]

Soul ties are God's design, as you will soon discover, unfortunately, the enemy always strives to pervert God's design, and this is no different. Soul ties are not limited to sexual interactions. They can also be enacted through vows/covenants, spiritual practices, trauma and abuse and deep emotional bonds. As we delve into the study of the system of sex, we focus solely on sexual relationship and their impact on your soul.

---

[2] Gordon, Christine. "What Is a Soul Tie? Here's Everything You Need to Know." *Brides*, 3 Nov. 2025, https://www.brides.com/soul-tie-explained-5498605

CHAPTER 1
LOSING MY VIRGINITY

Around 2007, I entered a situationship with a guy. This was only the second person that I had been with sexually, the first being a friend whom I had coerced to take my virginity due to some traumatic experiences.

While I was in college, two different men tried to rape me. Both experiences occurred in the presence of friends and even family. During one of the interactions, I was with one of my cousins. We had gone to a friend's house to hang out. I was doing my cousin's hair in his room, and when she stepped out of the room, he attacked me. I remember being confused but also screaming and fighting. Fighting so hard that I was bruised. Fighting so hard that the watch my mother gifted me somehow got pulled from my arm.

Finally, my cousin came back into the house, and he let me go. When I asked her why she did not come to intervene, because I knew she must have heard my screams; she replied that she thought my screams were an indication of "play". I am sure you can imagine the trauma.

In 2006, I decided to leave Florida, my safe space, away from trusted friends and family, to move to Louisiana. As a result of this move, I knew I had to make a drastic decision regarding my virginity. The lie the enemy, aka Satan, sold me was that the Lord protected me these two times; the third time, I would be on my own. Unfortunately, because these attempts had occurred with friends and family in the direct vicinity, this lie was completely believable. In my mind, the only logical thing to do was to break the promise I made to myself and God when I was a child and find someone to give my virginity to.

My twenty-year-old brain decided to have a trusted friend take my virginity because I could not fathom the pain of my first experience being taken from me. It amazes me at the things that make sense in the moment but later are revealed for the folly that they truly are when observed through the lens of wisdom.

I fell for the trap of the enemy hook, line, and sinker. I did exactly what he was baiting me to do: run towards sexual sin instead of away from it. Somehow, I thought I could save myself, protect myself, and keep myself from heartbreak. This could not have been further from the truth. I ran straight into the destruction I wanted to avoid. It just looked different. But I learned soon after, bondage is bondage.

After giving my virginity to my friend, I naïvely walked into the "situationship" with this new man. The first time we had sex, I went into depression. The kind where I was skipping class, and lying in bed all day, barely eating, and living under the weight of the pain and the shame of what I had allowed to happen. In my mind, yes, I had given away my virginity, but I was still not supposed to have sex again until my husband. The realization that not only had I had sex again, but that I had added a new name to my list almost broke me.

The thing with sin is that the more you do it, the more you become desensitized to it. The conviction is still there, just quieter, lower. For me, it was present, but I learned to live with it and ignore it to some degree. It was like the beeping sound of the dying battery of a smoke alarm. Sometimes it is not until someone asks, "What is that noise?" that you realize it has become a part of your life instead of doing what it was designed to do, alert you that something is dying.

That is the beauty of conviction. It is an alert system. It screams, "You are out of alignment! Something is dying! You are headed towards destruction! Turn around!" Unfortunately, a lot of us keep going until death has already started, and the smell of decay permeates the atmosphere.

The smell of self-hatred and depression. The smell of bitterness and rage. The smell of the inability to sleep. The addiction that keeps you living paycheck to paycheck. When we ignore God's alert system to turn from our wicked ways and return back to Him, a fragrance of death is always released.

Unfortunately, this situationship with this man did not end after the first time we slept together. In addition to a part of me slowly dying, I was also becoming someone I did not know or really like. I was starting to remind myself of this man, and there was a lot about him that I did not like. I could not really explain the attraction, even to myself.

It started becoming a problem when the things that I used to see present in him began manifesting in me. And not only manifesting in me, but a manifestation I had no control over. It was as if a war was raging in my soul and mind, and I was losing ground daily.

I am Haitian, and my entire church life, up until college was in the Haitian church. There, we were taught that sex was for marriage, but no one explained why you should not have sex before marriage. We were only told we were not supposed to do it. I had no idea about soul ties, and I certainly did not know about the biological and psychological ramifications of sex outside of marriage! I wish someone had told me. I would have RAN for my life. It now makes complete sense why scripture says to RUN from sexual immorality.

"Run from sexual sin! No other sin so clearly affects the body as this one does. For sexual immorality is a sin against your own body." I Corinthians 6:18 (NLT)

When it comes to sexual sin, Scripture does not instruct us to use the fruit of the Spirit. This is not an opportunity to test the strength of our self-control. This is not the time to use our spiritual gifts. There is no prophecy, tongues, or prayer needed. We are not instructed to test the spirit. Our discernment is not needed right now. We are told to R U N, RUN!

This one is not about the manifestation of God's spirit for someone else's sake; it is about protecting YOURSELF from destruction, because this is the one sin you commit against your body, not another person.

CHAPTER 2
THE COST OF SEX

I remember when I finally decided to stop having sex outside of marriage. I realized that every time I slept with someone, whether it was in the context of an established relationship or something else, it all ended the same way; with the feeling that I was some sort of a prostitute. I know it sounds crazy, but I always felt like they should be leaving some money on the nightstand.

Writing this book is helping me to recognize that this feeling was my mind's attempt to conceptualize what my soul was receiving at the time, which translated into these emotions: "Ludie, you are giving away something priceless That you are not getting back. They are walking away with a part of you, and there is a price on this exchange!" At the time, I theorized it as a monetary price, hence the nightstand thought pattern, but it was much deeper than I understood. I am truly receiving this revelation as I type this.

It is not only that there is a price for the exchange of sex, but there is only one acceptable currency for sex, and that is the covenant of marriage. People will say that they "love" you, to convince you to have sex with them, but love is not enough. That love needs to be placed within the boundaries of covenantal marriage to be an acceptable tender. Sufficiency only happens when two people are willing to pay the price of covenant and say, "I belong to you, and you belong to me, without restrictions or limitations until Jesus calls one of us home." Exclusively. THAT is the only acceptable allowance for sex.

I believe if we equip people with the knowledge as to the true ramifications of sex outside of marriage, the decision to run, abstain, and choose celibacy would be a lot more appealing. While culture celebrates sexual "freedom", what we are not being told is that sex outside of marriage results in bondage. People are having sex without calculating the effects on their souls. And there is a major effect.

Matthew 16:26 (NKJV) **says,** *"For what profit is it to a man if he gains the whole world, and loses his own soul? Or what will a man give in exchange for his soul?"*

We might think sex is all fun and games, but it comes at a cost to our souls. If you have purchased this book, you are probably realizing that you might be dealing with soul bankruptcy as a result of sex outside of marriage. What is being taken from us that we have not yet noticed? Maybe our identity, our sense of self-worth, or even the question of whether we are worth loving. How many of these false thoughts are a result of ungodly sexual relationships?

Jesus Himself clearly communicated who is controlling the airwaves in our society. He says in *John 14:30 (NKJV),* *"I will no longer talk much with you, for the ruler of this world is coming, and he has nothing in Me."*

And again, Apostle Paul reminds us in *Ephesians 2:2 (NKJV),* **which states,** *in which you once walked according to the course of this world, according to the prince of the* *power of the air, the spirit who now works in the sons of disobedience.*

What is being pushed out in culture is intentional by the one who desires our destruction. Satan, the devil, the enemy of our souls. He knows his eternity is signed, sealed, and delivered, but he wants to take as many of us with him as possible. He does this through lies, manipulation, and misinformation.

As I mentioned earlier, I realized that I started picking up this man's bad habits in this initial relationship. I was always a diligent student, but I started sleeping in, skipping class, and just not caring. I knew something was wrong, but I could not figure out what was going on with me. I was not praying like I am now, but I was asking God for help, and in His mercy, He led me to a sermon. I cannot recall the preacher, but I remember the man saying, if you slept with someone and you started taking on their habits and acting like them, you picked up their spirits, and you are dealing with a soul tie. That was the first time I had ever heard of soul ties, but he led us in a powerful prayer, and I started to get some relief, but I knew I was not fully free.

We are instructed in *I Corinthians 7:2-5 (NKJV),*

"Nevertheless, because of sexual immorality, let each man have his own wife, and let each woman have her own husband. Let the husband render to his wife the affection due her, and likewise also the wife to her husband. The wife does not have authority over her own body, but the husband does. And likewise the husband does not have authority over his own body, but the wife does. Do not deprive one another except with consent for a time, that you may give yourselves to fasting and prayer; and come together again so that Satan does not tempt you because of your lack of self-control."

Scripturally, a woman's body belongs to her husband, and her husband's body belongs to her. They have unlimited access to each other. This access backfires and becomes dangerous when we engage in sex outside of marriage. In marriage, our spouse has authority over our body, they know exactly what to do to get us to the place of desire, even if we are not initially in the mood. Sometimes, they do not even need to be in the room. One word, one look, one text will start something we did not expect. The danger of sex outside of marriage is that we consent to a sexual partner possessing the same level of access that is reserved for our spouse. Now this person has authority over our body, just without the covenant.

If you are honest with yourself, this explains why your body still yearns for past partners, and their memories affect you. Some of you may have experienced seeing these ex- partners in your dreams. It is as if you really cannot get away from them. Unfortunately, this inability to completely be free of past sexual partners does not only apply to singles; there are married men and women all over the world who are struggling. Struggling to understand why an ex is still on their mind when they are trying to be intimate with their spouse. Struggling to understand why their body responds at the thought of someone whom they have no affection for, but who seems bound to their soul. Wondering why this man or woman is showing up in their dreams even though they have moved on

CHAPTER 3
THE BIBLE AND SEX

Biblically, marriage is not just a ceremony; it is sex. Even in present day, you can annul a marriage if one of the partners is unable to perform their sexual duty, or if the marriage was never consummated. The lack of sex invalidates the marriage. It is not a divorce, it just gets erased, as if it never happened.

Genesis 2:24 (NKJV) **says,** *"Therefore a man shall leave his father and mother and be joined to his wife, and they shall become one flesh."*

I Corinthians 6:16 (NKJV) **echoes,** *"Or do you not know that he who is joined to a harlot is one* *body with her? For "the two," He says, "shall become one flesh."*

The two Bible verses I just referenced clearly explain what happens when sex is introduced. The fact is, once we have sex with someone, we become one flesh, and things that may have once only applied to them now apply to us.

Some of you may be dealing with financial issues that are not yours, but because of the person you engaged with sexually, because sex means becoming one, there was a transference. The mindsets, emotions, certain desires, and appetites that seemed to come out of nowhere can most likely be traced to a sexual partner. The scary thing is that it is not just them that you are dealing with, but also the people they slept with before you. That insecurity is not theirs or yours; it belongs to the girlfriend from three years ago who was never removed from his soul. What could we be picking up that we are not aware of as we choose to become one with this one, that one, and the other one too?

When the Holy Spirit instructed me to look up the biology behind sex, I was not ready for the research I found. My curiosity was first piqued to research what happens to sperm in the female body, only to be informed by Google that any sperm that was not expelled was "reabsorbed" into the woman's body. I was not expecting that answer. What in the world does that mean, "reabsorbed"? You mean to tell me it became a part of me? I am not sure what I expected, but this was not the answer I thought I would find.

The more research I conducted on the biology of sex, the clearer it became that scripture was spot on when it says you become one.

CHAPTER 4
THE SYSTEM OF SEX

God designed sex and marriage as a system that runs without His constant intervention. He does not need to remind our spouse to love us daily, to be loyal, to protect us to the point of putting their life on the line, to prefer our needs over their own. He built a system, through hormones, by way of sex, that brings us into oneness. A place of mutual preservation, where our success is their success. A place where we can trust one another fully, because He created us to be naked together and feel no shame –physically, emotionally, and spiritually.

But we have tried to scam the system. We have attempted to bypass God's design through "casual sex." The problem is, when the system is designed by the ultimate Creator, baby, it is going to work, and it is going to work well. That is why breakups feel different when sex is involved. It is not simply the end of a relationship; it feels like the death of a part of you. The grief you feel? That is mourning. The mourning is part of the design, because separation was never meant to come weeks after a hookup or a few months of dating. It was meant to come at death.

Sex in marriage is a sacrament of love, reinforced biologically by bonding hormones, emotionally by trust, and spiritually by covenant.

PART II
THE SCIENCE OF SOUL TIES: WHY SEX BINDS BODIES AND SOULS

Culture says sex can be fun, casual, non-committal, all about pleasure and liberating, but sex is deeper than all of those things. Sex is both biological and spiritual. Sadly, those who have suffered sexual abuse know firsthand the power sex has over a life. The act did not remain as a one-time event in the place where it occurred, it stays with the person long past the experience. It can manifest through fear, shame, depression and so many other ways that go beyond a momentary act. Sex changes lives forever.

As more scientific studies are conducted on sex and how the body reacts, it is clear that sex is more than pleasure. It is more than creating children. Sex is a bonding agent.

As much as I understand the spiritual ramifications of sex, the more I study the biological side, the more it reinforces the truth of God's word regarding sex. There is a cost. There is an exchange, and it is more than most people realize. To help illustrate how this affects both parties, we will study this from a male and female perspective.

CHAPTER 5
MEN AND SEX: DESIGNED TO CONNECT

We often focus on the female aspect of soul ties and connection, while completely ignoring the male. Culture has portrayed men as detached, sometimes unfeeling. Looking only to conquer and not connect, with no emotional cost to their sexual escapades, but science is revealing that this is in fact a lie.

Science confirms that men were created not to conquer, but to protect and connect with one woman through sex. God commands faithfulness in marriage, not because it is an impossible task, but because He put the ability in men. He would not create men with a desire to conquer women as opposed to the ability to connect with one woman but then command them to be faithful and not fornicate or commit adultery. The very call to monogamy is proof that we were created with fidelity in mind. Both men and women.

While men and women may respond differently to sex because God created us distinctly, it does not lessen the fact that there is a cost for men as well. It is not a wham- bam, thank you, ma'am situation. Men also create connections that affect their emotions, and most importantly, their souls. Their "body count" may be high, but with every person they add on, it is also leaving a count against them spiritually, emotionally, and hormonally.

I am by no means a scientist, but I will do my best to unpack three key chemicals that surge in men during sex: dopamine, oxytocin, and vasopressin. This will help us understand them and grasp the real biological impact on men, sex, and relationships.

Dopamine: The Reward Chemical[3]

When a man experiences an orgasm, he releases the chemical called dopamine, also known as the reward chemical. This chemical causes neurological and hormonal changes that hardwire emotional memory and behavioral patterns. You may have heard dopamine mentioned in connection with a warning. It is that rush you get from constantly scrolling on social media, or for those of us who love food; that feeling after the first bite of a warm, chewy chocolate chip cookie.

Sex also triggers the release of dopamine, activating the brain's reward system. The result is a "high" that creates a strong connection to the sexual partner. What is interesting with men is that this connection is not always limited to the partner, it often extends to the fantasy surrounding the moment and even the circumstances. The reason he keeps calling might not be because he loves her.

---

[3] *Kuhn, Simone, and Jürgen Gallinat. "Brain Structure and Functional Connectivity Associated with Pornography Consumption: The Brain on Porn." JAMA Psychiatry, vol. 71, no. 7, 2014, pp. 827–834*

He might not even want to be with her. He could simply be chasing that rush, that feeling he got when she did that thing, in that place.

In a marriage, this is sacred and special because it reinforces intimacy and satisfaction, creating beautiful memories between a husband and wife. This reward does not exist outside the context of marriage; instead, it becomes a trap. This is also how some men have become addicted to pornography; it is not just the act; it is also the context of the sex act and the desire it brings out in them.

Oxytocin: The Bonding Hormone[4]

Another hormone that affects men in connection to sex is oxytocin. This hormone is also called the "bonding hormone" or the "trust chemical". This is a chemical released during climax, but also during physical affection, so it does not even require an orgasm.

This chemical promotes emotional connection; it builds trust and increases vulnerability. While this

---

[4] Carter, C. Sue. "Neuroendocrine Perspectives on Social Attachment and Love." Psychoneuroendocrinology, vol. 23, no. 8, 1998, pp. 779–818.

chemical is found in higher quantities in women than men, it is still worth noting.

To the men reading this book: the more you have sex with her, the more vulnerable and trusting you become. When you study the story of Samson and Delilah and his downfall, you see that she does not simply pester him for the source of his strength, each time he sleeps with her, he becomes more emotionally exposed, more willing to trust, and ultimately more vulnerable.

Judges 16:19 (NKJV) **tells us,** *"Then she lulled him to sleep on her knees, and called for a man and had him shave off the seven locks of his head. Then she began to torment him, and his strength left him."*

Samson becomes so vulnerable and trusting of Delilah that she brings another man into the room, and he does not wake up. She then has that man shave his head, and still, he does not wake up. This is not merely a trim; we are talking about shaving. A sharp razor is rubbing his very scalp, and yet he sleeps through it. He is so lulled into deceptive trust, so emotionally entangled with Delilah, that he can no longer discern when there is a blade on his scalp. Even the loss of the weight of the locks he has carried his entire life does not alert him. He is awakened not by the absence of his strength, but by the torment of the one to whom he entrusted his soul.

Many have missed the signs and kept sleeping with an enemy because they convinced themselves they loved them. They convinced themselves this person was for them and that they would protect them when, in truth, they were planning their demise. They were cheating. They were badmouthing them to their friends. And yet, because they continued becoming one with them, the system kept working, and that became the source of their deceit.

It is not that the love is so deep they cannot walk away, it is also that the oxytocin that was built to work for them is now working against them. Oxytocin did its job and bound two people together, but now it is being told, "let go, we are moving on," but that is just bringing confusion to the system, and coincidentally, pain to the person.

These truths are encouraging in the context of marriage. Sex is protection. Sex is spiritual. It is emotional. It is physical. The more you do it with the one God has called you to, the better it gets. That is how the system is designed to function.

Luis and I are currently in our eighth year of marriage, and I can honestly say, our sex life gets better each year. The more I understand that sex is not just about physical intimacy, but also about becoming one spiritually, and now biologically, the clearer the command of scripture to keep coming together becomes. Thanks to oxytocin, my husband's level of trust and vulnerability grows every time we are intimate. Intimacy is important, but it is also about building trust, connection, and spiritual covering.

As *I Corinthians 7:5 (NKJV)* **says,** *"Do not deprive one another except with consent for a time, that you may give yourselves to fasting and prayer; and come together again so that Satan does not tempt you because of your lack of self-control."*

Every time Luis and I come together, our connection grows. Our communication, his ability to trust me and be honest with me also increases. Men, this is something that is too sacred to lay at any woman's feet because she is "beautiful" or "sexy".

When oxytocin is released, it takes two people and binds them together. There are some betrayals, heartaches, and wounds that would not have been experienced if sex had never entered the picture.

Vasopressin: The Loyalty Hormone[5]

I have heard people argue that men are not built for monogamy, that God created them to "spread their seed." However, both science and Scripture tell a very different story.

> *"Nevertheless, because of sexual immorality, let each man have his own wife, and let each woman have her own husband." -1 Corinthians 7:2 (NKJV)*

After sex, vasopressin, often called the "monogamy molecule" floods the male brain. This powerful neuropeptide drives deep connection, sparking feelings of attachment, possessiveness, and a strong sense of responsibility toward one's partner.

Sadly, we have all heard stories of men becoming possessive of women, treating them as possessions rather than people. While there is a myriad of contributing factors to this behavior, sex is often one

---

[5] Lim, Miranda M., and Larry J. Young. "Neuropeptidergic Regulation of Affiliative Behavior in Animals." Hormones and Behavior, vol. 50, no. 4, 2006, pp. 506–517.

of them. So many heartbreaking scenarios could have been avoided if the line of sex had not been crossed. God created man to desire and to be attached to his wife, not a girlfriend, not a one-night stand.

God created men to be attached to one woman and to desire to protect her. Men are not made to conquer; they are made to cover. This perfectly aligns with the Scripture's call for men to serve as the head and priest of their household, *"For the husband is head of the wife, as also Christ is head of the church; and He is the Savior of the body" Ephesians 5:23 (NKJV).*

Culture presents one narrative about sex, while God and science paint a different picture. When a man engages in casual sex, the chemical system God designed still activates. The body does not distinguish between casual sex and marital sex. It does what it was created to do. Therefore, when a man engages in casual sex, dopamine, oxytocin, and vasopressin are still released. But outside of commitment, those bonds break, leading to confusion, guilt, and soul trauma. Sex imprints her on his brain, as well as his soul. The fact that some men may not communicate this does not lessen the truth of God's word and science.

From the beginning, God created us for a covenant.

"That is why a man leaves his father and mother and is united to his wife, and they become one flesh." Genesis 2:24 (NIV)

God did not create men to be predators; He created them to be protectors.

Husbands, love your wives, just as Christ loved the church and gave himself up for her to make her holy, cleansing her by the washing with water through the word, and to present her to himself as a radiant church, without stain or wrinkle or any other blemish, but holy and blameless. In this same way, husbands ought to love their wives as their own bodies. He who loves his wife loves himself." Ephesians 5:25-28 (NIV)

As a woman, I was absolutely floored to discover the biological effects of sex on men. Because of my own personal experiences, this has shed a lot of light on some lingering questions. The deeper I have gotten into this project, the clearer it has become that this is as much for me, as it is for you, the reader.

I have always had a natural understanding of the female sexual experience, largely because I have lived it. However, gaining insight into the male experience through a scientific and spiritual lens has deepened my appreciation for God's intentional design.

CHAPTER 6
WOMEN AND SEXUAL BONDING

As we have already seen, culture and the Word of God operate from two very different frameworks when it comes to sex. But when we add science to the conversation, it only confirms what Scripture has already made clear: sex is not just a physical act. It is a moment of oneness, a becoming that happens simultaneously, purposefully, and powerfully. It is deeply spiritual, emotional, and hormonal, especially for women.

From hormone absorption (yes, women actually take in some of a man's DNA) to immune responses, sex activates sacred chemistry that goes far beyond the moment itself. The act may end, but there is continuation within the woman's body, mind, and soul.[6]

In this chapter we examine how sex influences the female body, mind, and soul, and why God's design for sexual intimacy within marriage is both beautiful and profoundly protective. His plan is not restrictive. It is intentional. It is powerful. And it is rooted in love.

Oxytocin: The Bonding Hormone

Like men, women also release the hormone oxytocin during sex, especially at the point of orgasm. Often called the "Cuddle hormone," oxytocin increases emotional trust and strengthens attachment. As unbelievable as it may seem, oxytocin also gets released at another marking time for women. Get this, it is the same hormone released during childbirth and breastfeeding.[7] That is how powerful this bond is. The

---

[6] Schjenken, John E., and Sarah A. Robertson. "Seminal Fluid Signaling in the Female Reproductive Tract: Implications for Reproductive Success and Offspring Health." Frontiers in Immunology, vol. 11, 2020, p. 356.

[7] Gallup, Gordon G., Jr., et al. "Does Semen Function as an Antidepressant?" Archives of Sexual Behavior, vol. 31, 2002, pp. 289–293.

very hormone that bonds a mother to her baby is released during sex. Sex, then, cannot be casual; it is always sacred.

Now, I have not yet born any children, but the way I feel bonded to my nieces gives me a glimpse of what my sister must experience. It is beyond me to fully grasp that God designed sex to bond me to my husband with the same depth and intensity. A child spends nine months inside the mother, drawing nourishment, protection, and care. That is the level of intimacy and trust God wants us to experience with the person we are covenanted to in marriage.

It now makes complete sense why I used to feel so cheap after sex when it was out of the covenant of marriage. Sex was designed as a vehicle to build trust, deepen attachment, and create bonding between two people who are giving themselves fully to each other. But when that person is not your spouse, the design still activates, the bond still forms, but the context is broken.

Oxytocin does not ask if he is your husband. It does not wait to check if he loves you, respects you, or intends to stay. It simply binds you to the one you are with. The system is working exactly as it was designed. The issue is not with the system, it is that we have stepped outside of God's alignment.

Oxytocin does not discern how he makes you feel, or whether he is worthy of your trust. It only knows how to do its job: to connect, to attach, and to bond. And it does it very well. There is no thought of how the aftermath will play out. There is no logic, simply obedience to the system. Just like a good working computer. It is following the code it has been programmed to.

Dopamine: The Pleasure Reinforcer

Women also experience the release of dopamine during sex. This hormone functions as a reward chemical, linking pleasurable experiences with the person involved.[8] In a covenant marriage, this system serves as a gift from God. It reinforces the joy and intimacy between husband and wife, making sexual unity not only revered but deeply satisfying.

Dopamine trains the brain to crave more of what feels good. It bonds the pleasure of the act to the person,

---

[8] Cera, Natascia, et al. "How Relevant Is the Systemic Oxytocin Concentration for Human Sexual Behavior? A Systematic Review." Sexual Medicine, vol. 9, 2021, p. 100370.

encouraging repeated connection.8 In marriage, this system supports God's design for ongoing unity, not just physically, but emotionally and spiritually.

As **1** *Corinthians 7:5 (NKJV)* **says,** *"Do not deprive each other except perhaps by mutual consent and for a time, so that you may devote yourselves to prayer. Then come together again so that Satan will not tempt you because of your lack of self-control."*

This is God's design to protect the union and guard against temptation by strengthening the marital bond through consistent intimacy.

Outside of the marriage covenant, dopamine becomes a double-edged sword. What God designs to deepen healthy attachment now drives unhealthy obsession. It rewards the brain for an experience that may be spiritually damaging or emotionally unsafe. Even when the relationship is toxic or clearly out of alignment with God's will, dopamine pulls you back because your brain is being trained to crave it.

This is why many people feel stuck in sexual sin or emotionally entangled in relationships they know are wrong. The body feels pleasure, and dopamine reinforces the behavior, regardless of whether it aligns with the truth, His truth. The chemical system functions exactly as God designed it, but when misused, it leads us astray.

When pleasure disconnects from purpose, dopamine becomes a powerful tool of deception. What should build intimacy and trust in marriage instead binds us to counterfeit connections. The same system that God intends to bless us works against us when we step outside of His covering.

Dopamine exists to make marital intimacy life-giving and joy-filled, not to chain us to emotionally damaging or spiritually empty relationships. When we honor God's boundaries, the brain's reward system serves as part of our protection. But outside of His will, it reinforces patterns that break us.

Vasopressin: The Loyalty Molecule

Vasopressin is another hormone that both men and women share. Although more dominant in men, women also release vasopressin. In women, it contributes to emotional security, bonding after sex, and births a desire for exclusivity and protection[9].

Vasopressin causes a woman to bypass wisdom and reality due to its response and effects on their emotions. It makes them loyal despite. It tells them that they are emotionally safe, even though the actions towards them speak to the contrary. It compels them to want this person for themselves and them alone.

Vasopressin will cause a woman to play the role of a wife at the expense of herself to ensure that the man chooses her above anyone else. Vasopressin will cause a woman to disregard how she is spoken to or treated. It causes them to hold on tightly with no desire to ever let go.

---

[9] Taylor, Shelley E., et al. "Are Plasma Oxytocin in Women and Plasma Vasopressin in Men Biomarkers of Distressed Pair-Bond Relationships?" Psychological Science, vol. 21, no. 1, 2010, pp. 3–7

CHAPTER 7
SEMEN ABSORPTION: HORMONAL & BIOLOGICAL IMPACT

What started me down this rabbit hole of research was a simple question: What happens to semen in a woman? I just stared at the screen when Google calmly informed me that it is reabsorbed into the body. What do you mean? Well, you are about to get that answer.

Semen is not as simple as what it is commonly known as, merely sperm. Semen contains more than simply sperm; it also includes hormones like testosterone, prostaglandins, cortisol, and immune-modulating proteins.

I am sure you are wondering, what in the world does that mean, Ludie? Well, for one, these molecules are absorbed through the vaginal walls and enter the bloodstream. Yes, the same bloodstream that flows to all your organs. As scripture advises, you truly become one flesh.

Additionally, seminal fluid triggers the immune system to prepare for possible conception, so the woman's body goes into nesting mode. Studies suggest that this exposure may affect mood, immune regulation, and hormonal balance because of the signals that are sent to the woman's body.[10] In a woman, semen is a signal to prepare to connect, protect, and possibly conceive. The body does not distinguish casual sex; it was built to submit to and assist in covenantal biology to bring about life. I will keep saying this: the system was created to work, and it does!

---

[10] Schjenken, John E., and Sarah A. Robertson. "Seminal Fluid Signaling in the Female Reproductive Tract: Implications for Reproductive Success and Offspring Health." Frontiers in Immunology, vol. 11, 2020, p. 356.

Are you starting to understand how soul ties are formed? This is much more than an emotional entanglement; it is a soul entrapment. Any connection we form in the natural realm is minimal compared to the connection made in the spiritual realm. For example, let us look at pregnancy. Getting pregnant in the natural realm is a physical manifestation of a life sent to the earth. Even before a woman is aware she is pregnant, eternity has already been sent forth.

"He has made everything beautiful in its time. He has also set eternity in the human heart; yet no one can fathom what God has done from beginning to end." –Ecclesiastes 3:11(NIV)

God does not send babies to the earth; He sends men and women wrapped around destiny and purpose. Meaning, the form in which something is presented is not a representation of its totality. We see a cute baby, God sees a man He sent to the earth to proclaim His word, marry, have children, and work as an accountant to help financially fund the kingdom of God, who loves travelling and cooking. In our limited human view, what we see as a child is already in their eternal form and assignment in the eyes of heaven.

The fullness of who God has called them to be in the spirit.

There is no junior Holy Spirit. Let's take a deeper look at this through Scripture:

"Listen to me, you islands; hear this, you distant nations: Before I was born the Lord called me; from my mother's womb he has spoken my name. He made my mouth like a sharpened sword, in the shadow of his hand he hid me; he made me into a polished arrow and concealed me in his quiver. He said to me, "You are my servant, Israel, in whom I will display my splendor." But I said, "I have labored in vain; I have spent my strength for nothing at all. Yet what is due me is in the Lord's hand, and my reward is with my God." And now the Lord says – he who formed me in the womb to be his servant to bring Jacob back to him and gather Israel to himself, for I am honored in the eyes of the Lord and my God has been my strength – he says: "It is too small a thing for you to be my servant to restore the tribes of Jacob and bring back those of Israel I have kept. I will also make you a light for the Gentiles, that my salvation may reach to the ends of the earth." This is what the Lord says – the Redeemer and Holy One of Israel – to him who was

*despised and abhorred by the nation, to the servant
of rulers: "Kings will see you and stand up, princes
will see and bow down, because of the Lord , who is
faithful, the Holy One of Israel, who has chosen
you." –Isaiah 49:1-7 (NIV)*

What a powerful prophetic word and life changing destiny! This scripture, clearly illustrates that Prophet Isaiah's assignment was established from the womb, not at a certain point in his life or at a particular age. There is no catalyst; there is only genesis. He is sent to the earth with all the attributes needed to complete the will and destiny God has placed inside of him.

What am I getting at? What we see and experience physically is only a small glimpse of a much greater spiritual reality. With that in mind, when God says that sex makes us "one flesh," and science continues to uncover evidence that confirms what God has already declared, how deep does this really go? How much are we still unaware of when it comes to the mystery and sacredness of sex?

In sex, the biochemical bonding and hormonal absorption contribute to the formation of soul ties. The reality is that soul ties are not a negative occurrence; the issue is that your soul is only created to be bound to one until death. A soul tie is a beautiful thing when the prescribed boundary is respected. It is our own free will that gives a soul tie a negative connotation.

Our free will to bind to multiple partners gives us access to unhealthy emotional ties that only perpetuate toxic cycles.

It invites confusion, anxiety, or depression after breakups. It becomes difficult to separate emotionally, even when we are mentally ready to leave. By giving our body away, our soul interprets this as confirmation that we are safe, that this is forever, and that we must attach to this person. Sex was never meant to happen outside the context of marriage. It was created to unify you with one person, body, soul, and spirit.

Sex is powerful. So powerful that God had to confine it in a covenant to keep it from breaking our souls.

Picture this: you are in a rush and realize you have forgotten an important document by the front door. Now your car is parked a couple of feet away, and you know you can run quickly inside to grab this document. You leave the car running and run inside, only to get outside to find your car speeding away from your house.

The car is doing its job and driving that individual to where they want to go. To the car, it does not care that it has been stolen from its rightful owner. You. It does not know if it is a child driving, an elderly person, or a criminal, it does not matter. The car is not going to stop simply because you are not in the driver's seat, but the thief will face repercussions.

The same is true with sex. It was designed to work, however, using it in the wrong context or with the wrong person will bring negative repercussions. Sex is not the problem; God made it beautiful, but boundaries matter. *Song of Songs 8:4 (NIV)* speaks to this directly, *"Daughters of Jerusalem, I charge you: Do not arouse or awaken love until it so desires."*

All these hormones were given to us to keep us married. To find healing, strength, safety and to keep us attached to each other despite what may happen in our marriages. The issue that arises is when we are trying to attach to someone who is not our spouse, or worse, the relationship is toxic, but we become stuck. Not stuck simply because we love them, or feel duty-bound, but also because our very biology is at war and in conflict because of the divine design of sex.

CHAPTER 8
SEX AND CONFLICT

During my research, I came across a paper titled "Are Plasma Oxytocin in Women and Plasma Vasopressin in Men Biomarkers of Distressed Pair-Bond Relationships?" Written by Shelley E. Taylor, Shimon Saphire-Bernstein, and Teresa E. Seeman University of California, Los Angeles. Their research absolutely astounded me

As I read through this document, I found myself thinking, "Wait a minute now! Am I understanding this correctly?" In scripture, it says that the angels around the throne cry "Holy, holy, holy is the Lord God almighty," and reading this paper literally had me meditating on the wisdom and power of God and caused me to cry "HOLY! The way He has built the body to abide by and obey His word is simply marvelous.

To sum up the research, they discovered the following:

1. In women, plasma oxytocin was significantly associated with distress in pair-bond relationships... including verbal conflict, disappointment, and perceived criticism.

2. In men, vasopressin was significantly associated with emotional distress in their romantic relationships.

In short, the same hormones that are released during sex to bind you together also get released when you are in conflict, especially in attachment-related distress, to bring you back together.[9] In toxic relationships, frequent stress, rejection, or inconsistent affection elevate key bonding hormones, not just any hormones, but higher plasma oxytocin levels in women and Vasopressin in men[9]. In toxic relationships, frequent stress, rejection, or inconsistent affection elevate key bonding hormones, not just any hormones, but higher plasma oxytocin levels in women and Vasopressin in men[9]. The study describes this as a neuroendocrine response to threat or distress in a relationship[11].

On the next page, you will find a chart that further breaks down the results of the study. Here is a chart to explain this better:

---

[11] Young, Larry J., and Thomas R. Insel. "The Neurobiology of Pair Bonding." Nature Neuroscience, vol. 7, no. 10, 2004, pp. 1048–1054.

11Hormone	Gender	Effect During Sex	Triggers	Effect in Toxic Relationship
Oxytocin	Women	Strong bonding, trust, emotional closeness, desire for connection and security.	Conflict, Criticism, Insecurity	Oxytocin rises during emotional pain or conflict, increasing the urge to reconnect and feel seen, even in harmful situations. Can cause women to feel emotionally bonded to unhealthy partners.
Oxytocin	Men	Moderate bonding, enhances emotional intimacy and affectionate behavior.		Oxytocin still encourages bonding but can reinforce attachment to conflict when sex is used to resolve tension, leading to emotional confusion.
Vasopressin	Women	Mild emotional regulation, may support pair bonding but less active than in men.		Limited role in women, but may contribute to increased sensitivity to partner behavior. Less studied than oxytocin but can still support unhealthy attachment patterns.

11Hormone	Gender	Effect During Sex	Triggers	Effect in Toxic Relationship
Vasopressin	Men	Triggers protectiveness, territorial attachment, loyalty to partner, and bonding reinforcement.	Emotional tension, disconnection	Vasopressin increases with relational stress, intensifying fixation and territorial patterns. possessiveness, emotional Can deepen the trauma bond, making it harder to detach despite conflict.

In His infinite wisdom, God's divine design for sex is that it would bring a couple back together when they are not getting along, when they are hurting, angry, anxious or disappointed. When life and stress want to pull them apart, the desire for intimacy is part of the mechanism created to keep bringing them back together. The higher the stress and the more reasons not to come together, the louder the hormones scream, "Get back together!" This, of course, opens up an entire new realm of inquiry into sexless marriages. This confirms that the phenomenon of a sexless marriage is a direct attack from hell, and not just because life gets busy or a lack of desire, because it bypasses the system. But this is a conversation for another day, or in this case, another book.

These hormones are gifts from God designed to drive reconnection during conflict, which, within marriage, promotes healing, emotional repair, and a sense of safety. But, in a toxic, non-marital sexual relationship, what is meant to work for you is now working against you.

Whether married or not, when there is conflict with a sexual partner, the body still releases these chemicals in response to distress, driving toward reconnection.

In marriage, this brings two people back together to rebuild, but outside of marriage, this drives a person back to the one they should be running from. The craving for relief becomes confused with craving the person, and sex becomes a quick fix; a momentary release that does not bring restoration. The body may be bonding, but the spirit is breaking. This is not love. It is captivity.

After the fight, the gaslighting, the silent treatment, or the emotional rejection, the body seeks connection to soothe the pain. Women release oxytocin and men release vasopressin, both sending out urgent and loud demands: "Reattach! Reconnect! Make it Better!" Sex and physical intimacy become the path the body takes to escape the emotional tension. Instead of fleeing the pain, you end up running toward its source.

This may manifest as make-up sex, apologizing even when you did nothing wrong, or any attempt to be physically close to regain the deceptive illusion of love and connection. The more painful the relationship becomes, the more the body tries to fix it. Fix it through bonding hormones meant to protect the covenant, now misused in dysfunction. This is not true intimacy. It is a chemical coping mechanism, designed by God for marital restoration, now hijacked by trauma and pain. Oxytocin and vasopressin, designed by God for covenantal bonding, instead reinforce emotional addiction. The very thing God intended to heal through attachment in marriage is now being weaponized by dysfunction. It leads to bondage.

The issue is that the false reconnection and reattachment does work, temporarily. The physical connection pacifies the hormone spike (stress response), giving a false sense of safety and peace. The nervous system calms, but the trauma remains. Regrettably, this will only cement the cycle, not heal the trauma. When the cycle repeats, each round makes the bond more chemically and emotionally entrenched, not because of love, but because of survival. This is toxicity at its finest.

You find yourself hating how this person makes you feel, but returning to them to feel better. And that moment of relief tricks you into believing you are still loved and wanted. What culture may call passion may be hormones trying to pacify pain.

The study confirms, "The same hormones that sustain emotional bonding also appear to mediate distress during relationship strain."[9]

Because the body equates reconnection with safety, it deepens the emotional attachment over time. The longer the cycle continues, the harder it becomes to leave. You begin depending on the one causing your pain to also be your source of comfort.

This is the scientific mechanism behind trauma bonding, a pattern often seen in emotionally abusive or codependent relationships.

The woman's body floods with oxytocin, not just in moments of love, but also in the heat of chaos. The man's body is flooded with vasopressin, not only in intimacy, but when he is trying to retain control. The bond is not built on love or trust; it is built on trauma. Both bodies, in their own ways, are trying to fix it. Not through wisdom or truth, but the only way they know, by holding on tighter. This means that the same chemicals that form bonds in love can also tighten chains in dysfunction.

God designed sex and bonding hormones to unite two wholes, committed people in covenant, not to bind a broken soul to another wounded or abusive one.

Many Christians understand the spiritual dangers of sex outside of marriage but often underestimate its emotional and biological effects. The Bible's warning and prescription to run from sexual immorality might seem extreme, but once there is understanding of what occurs in the brain and soul, it makes complete sense. Outside of a covenant, the bonding hormones misfire. Instead of bringing unity, they bring confusion.

In connection with sex, one of the enemy's biggest traps for this generation is pornography and masturbation.

PART III
PORNOGRAPHY AND MASTURBATION: MY TESTIMONY

In addition to sex, pornography and masturbation are two other areas where we have also failed to equip the church with knowledge and strategy. You might ask, "What is wrong with masturbation spiritually? It is just me. I am not involving anyone else." But spiritually, that is false. It is just you and your imagination... except, what you are unaware of, is that you are opening spiritual gates and doors.

My church has a deliverance ministry called Soul Care. This ministry is based on the book Soul Care: 7 Transformational Principles for a Healthy Soul by Dr. Rob Reimer. I recommend that every person read this book. I 1000% recommend it –it has changed my life, my husband's life, and countless others.

My husband and I went through Soul Care and experienced freedom from bondages we did not even know were there. I also had the opportunity to attend one of Dr. Rob's three-day Soul Care Conferences back in June of 2025. If you have a chance to go, do it. It is worth every financial sacrifice. Your future, and generations after you, will thank you.

After the conference, I headed straight to the airport, and something strange happened. A man walked by, and I felt a "zap" on my clitoris. Now, this had happened before, but I had always rebuked it and kept moving. Now, having just come from deliverance, I thought I was free. I started to feel discouraged, but I knew better than to stay in that place. So, I asked the Lord what was going on.

He gently reminded me that although I had repented of pornography, lust, and many other things, I had never repented of masturbation. In addition to repenting for masturbation, I also never took the next step, which is to close the spiritual doors it had opened in my body. In essence, this open door provided the enemy a legal door with which to access and oppress me in that area. I am always humbled at the way God responds when we truly ask a question and listen for the response. All of these years, I had dealt with this issue and did not bring it to Him until that moment.

I cannot help but wonder how many years of freedom I missed out on because I never asked. It is not as if I did not know the bible verse connected to asking, I just never put it into action. Could this be your story as well?

Matthew 7:7 (NKJV) "Ask, and it will be given to you; seek, and you will find; knock, and it will be opened to you."

Now possessing this key of freedom, I immediately repented of masturbation and shut the door I had opened. To my surprise and relief, freedom came immediately. I cannot express how amazing it felt to be free of this bondage.

In that same moment in the airport, the Lord healed me from another area of struggle. There were times I would be in conversation with someone and suddenly get a vision of me making out with them. It was strange, disturbing, and made no sense. Again, at the airport, this happened again. But now I understood, God was allowing it to come to the surface so He could fully deliver me.

When I asked Him, "ok, how do I shut this door?", He reminded me of something else: I used to read erotic novels. He revealed to me I gave the enemy access to my imagination through these pictures and fantasies I entertained. God showed me that I had to not only repent but revoke every point of access the enemy had to my imagination.

See, what God revealed was this: the enemy had legal right to defile my imagination because I was the first to invite him in. Our imaginations are one of the ways God communicates with us. That is why the scripture urges us to guard our heart, and be mindful to meditate on what is good as it states in *Philippians 4:8 (NIV), "Finally, brothers and sisters, whatever is true, whatever is noble, whatever is right, whatever is pure, whatever is lovely, whatever is admirable – if anything is excellent or praiseworthy – think about such things."*

Your thoughts matter. They shape you more than you realize. You can only act on what you have already permitted in your heart. A thought is not just "a thought", it signals the intention of your soul.

We must wake up to the reality that we are spirit beings living in physical bodies. We say it, but do we actually grasp what that means? We occupy two realms at once and we must embrace this truth and its implications. Sexual immorality is not just about physical actions, it includes what happens in our minds. Purity starts within and flows outward.

"But I say to you that whoever looks at a woman to lust for her has already committed adultery with her in his heart." — Matthew 5:28 (NKJV)

CHAPTER 9
PORNOGRAPHY AND YOUR BRAIN

Science continues to confirm what Scripture has been saying all along. Repeated exposure to pornography literally rewires the brain. It links the release of dopamine, intended to bond us in intimacy and connection, to images, not people. Instead of anchoring us in connection, pornography confuses the system and causes a desire for novelty over intimacy, image over personhood, and temporary pleasure over covenant purpose.

This is not my opinion –it is backed by research. A 2014 study showed that pornography reduces gray matter in key areas of the brain[3]. In other words, extensive exposure to pornography physically alters the brain. Are you picking up what I am putting down? Not just our emotions, but the actual matter in our brains. Over time, pornography desensitizes the reward system, thereby making real-life intimacy harder to experience and sustain.

This is something I experienced first-hand. I was single for five years prior to my husband. Single and celibate. The Lord took me through a process of preparation, cleansing and restoration. I had a lot of junk He had to work on during that season. In that season is when I had my first supernatural deliverance from pornography. I used to be addicted. I mean in the sense that I would spend hours in my room watching pornography and masturbating. It felt as if it consumed my life.

During that season, we had a young adults service at my church and one of the nights, the pastor released a key that gave me my freedom. In essence, he said, when you do the thing that makes you hate yourself, declare your identity louder than the act. Say, "I am the righteousness of God in Christ Jesus." Quoting,

II Corinthians 5:21 (NKJV) For He made Him who knew no sin to be sin for us, that we might become the righteousness of God in Him.

In 2015 I had a five-hour pornography binge. I got off the bed, sat on my chaise and wept before the Lord. The sermon was fresh in my heart, and I just kept repeating those words over, and over again, "I am the righteousness of God in Christ Jesus." I cannot recall how long this went on, but I know that the desire left me after that moment. I have not watched pornography since, or desired to read an erotic novel. This was over a decade ago now. However, I did not yet know that though the spirit of pornography had been kicked out of the house of my heart, he had left some junk behind that I needed to clean up.

Once Luis and I got married and started becoming intimate, there would be moments where pornographic scenes from my past would sneak in. There were times it sometimes felt like those scenes were a door that I had to pass through in order to get the desire to be intimate with my husband. I had no idea what had happened to my brain. I just knew the enemy was defiling our marriage bed and I honestly did not know how to get past this, and this was not something people were openly discussing. This struggle stayed between me, Luis and the Lord.

I would say this would be an on and off battle for at least five years. It was not continuous, but it would undeniably occur enough to alert me to the fact that I was not yet free.

This part is going to be controversial, but this is my testimony. Around year five of our marriage, the Lord started putting a question in my heart about oral sex. It just felt like there was no clarity on if this was an act I should be participating in or not. I mentioned it to Luis, and it was just something we kept in prayer. Then the Lord answered. He gave me an instruction to start reading the book of Leviticus. In that act of obedience, I received my deliverance.

Leviticus 15:16-18 ''If any man has an emission of semen, then he shall wash all his body in water, and be unclean until evening. And any garment and any leather on which there is semen, it shall be washed with water, and be unclean until evening. Also, when a woman lies with a man, and there is an emission of semen, they shall bathe in water, and be unclean until evening.'

What the Lord said to me is if semen physically touching you caused you to be unclean until evening, how much more unclean would you be if it went into your mouth.

He further said that in order for this defilement and attack to stop in my marriage bed, I needed to remove every act from there that I had acquired from pornography. Now, Luis and I were not acting out pornography scenes, but had I never seen a man place his penis in a woman's mouth in pornography, it would have NEVER entered my mind that this was an ok thing to do. There were other ideas that I had also picked up from pornography that the Lord said they needed to go as well.

I spoke to Luis about it and he agreed that we should follow the conviction of the Lord and stop these acts. The change was IMMEDIATE. I mean, our sex life went from 80 to 1,000. Not only were the pornographic images gone, but the pleasure and the ability to be present just made everything more beautiful and enjoyable.

Luis later mentioned was that prior to this, there would be times when we were intimate and he would notice and feel that I was distant and by God's grace, we were free from this.

It might sound crazy, but this is our testimony, and I can confirm that I have shared this with others who have taken these steps, and they also noticed dramatic changes in their sex life.

God can do for you what He did for me. One thing I am now, is intentional. I am intentional about what I watch and listen to. As scripture advises, we are to guard our hearts.

Proverbs 4:23 (NLT) **says,** *"Guard your heart above all else, for it determines the course of your life."*

We cannot be people who continue to break our own hearts and wonder why we remain bound. We have to first choose freedom. In different parts of the scriptures, when people would come to Jesus, He would first ask, "What do you want me to do for you?" They had to first decide to go to Him. You also have a part to play in getting your freedom and maintaining.

John 5:14 (NKJV) Afterward Jesus found him in the temple, and said to him, "See, you have been made well. Sin no more, lest a worse thing come upon you."

CHAPTER 10
FREEDOM IN JESUS

You might be reading this with thanksgiving, for the understanding and the freedom you are receiving simply through the revelation of the truth, and that is beautiful. But God desires your complete freedom.

Maybe you are just now realizing you are not crazy for missing someone who hurt or abused you. You understand now that your oxytocin might be louder than your logic. If you are a man, maybe it is your vasopressin. Outside the covenant of marriage, the very system of hormones that formed a bond with someone can also be the very ones holding you hostage to that same person, regardless of your desire for freedom.

This project was originally meant to be a prayer for breaking soul ties. But armed with deeper knowledge, I now understand why the Lord asked me to dig deeper than I thought I knew.

These studies may not offer all the solutions, but we know through Scripture who does. His name is Jesus. And He finishes what He starts.

> *Galatians 5:1 (NIV)* **says,** *"It is for freedom that Christ has set us free. Stand firm, then, and do not let yourselves be burdened again by a yoke of slavery."*

For some of you, God may ask you to fast as you do this prayer over a period, in addition to other instructions. For others, doing this prayer once may be enough. You will need to seek His face for your specific plan. Some of you may need therapy. Perhaps God will recommend a detox from the opposite sex for a season to recalibrate your body, soul, and spirit. Consider a time of consecration; just you and Jesus. I was completely single for five years before God sent Luis, and I am so grateful I had that time to heal.

You may be sharing the same space as the person you need to separate from. I know how hard that can be because I have been there. I have lived with someone while trying to detox from them. I understand the weight of that burden, but I can promise you this: your soul is worth the cost, even financially. Ask God for wisdom on how to leave.

As I continue to emphasize, sex is not simply a physical act. It is a deeply spiritual, emotional, and chemically sacred exchange. When honored within marriage, it becomes a source of deep joy and lifelong connection. When misused, it often leaves behind invisible wounds. But God is the Healer of both body and soul, and His design still leads to freedom.

God gave me a prayer on spiritual divorce years ago, but with everything He has revealed since, it has been extended to cover the spiritual, emotional and biological portions of sex. You may find that these are prayers you need to return to more than once, and that is ok. Do not allow that to discourage you. Everyone's journey is different, and the Lord will give you any additional instructions you need along the way. Again, for some of you, God may lead you to fast through these prayers, just as Jesus taught, to ensure you experience a complete breakthrough.

> As Mark 9:29 (NKJV) **says,** *"So He said to them, 'This kind can come out by nothing but prayer and fasting."*

In addition to the prayer for freedom from soul ties, you will also find a prayer for those of you who may be battling pornography and masturbation. Just like the other prayer, you may have to do this one more than once, and some of you may have to fast. There is a level of desperation that is required to access freedom. You have to be desperate enough to do whatever it takes. No matter how inconvenient the process may be, or how long it can take. Freedom is the number one objective.

PART IV
DO YOU KNOW JESUS?

I t would be remiss of me to assume that everyone who picks up this book knows Jesus. No matter where you are in your faith journey, I pray that the information has been beneficial to you. Unfortunately, information is not enough; I believe that you need to add Jesus to the information in order to fully experience true freedom and deliverance.

If you do not know Jesus, I can tell you that He is the best thing that has ever happened to me. He is my Lord, my Savior, my Master, my healer, and everything I have ever needed.

He is God, and yet He chose to come as a man to pay the price that you and I could not pay. Our good works could not save us, nor could our good intentions.

At the basic level, Jesus is the Son of God, who came to earth in the form of a man and was killed, though completely innocent, in order to take on all our sins and shame. He died so we can live eternally with Him. He lived a completely sinless life and received the penalty of pain, shame, humiliation and the death that we deserved.

> John 3:16-17 NKJV 'For God so loved the world that He gave His only begotten Son, that whoever believes in Him should not perish but have everlasting life. For God did not send His Son into the world to condemn the world, but that the world through Him might be saved.'

I do not know your journey, but I can guarantee that He can save you like He did me, and restore your life to better than you can imagine. If you want to do some research on Jesus, that is ok. Grab a Bible and start reading the book of John. That is a good starting place. Simply ask Him to reveal Himself to you. You will be surprised at what you begin to see. If you want to accept Him into your heart, just pray this simple prayer out loud.

Dear Jesus, thank you for dying on the cross for my sins so that I may receive salvation through your blood. I confess that I am a sinner and that I will perish without you. Your word says in Romans 10:9 (NKJV) 'that if you confess with your mouth the Lord Jesus and believe in your heart that God has raised Him from the dead, you will be saved.

I confess with my mouth that Jesus Christ is the Son of God, that He died and God raised Him from the dead on the third day, and He now sits at the right hand of the Father. By reason of this confession and the belief in my heart, I receive salvation.

Please change me, mold me, and help me to live out the plans and purposes you have for my life. Help me to look more like you, Jesus. Amen.

CONGRATULATIONS! If this is your first time praying that prayer, welcome to the family. If you have prayed it before, welcome back to the family. For your next steps, I suggest finding a bible believing and preaching church and getting into community. We are better together, and we can go further in the community.

EPOLIGUE
SPIRITUAL DIVORCE PRAYER

T his prayer is meant to be read out loud. Find a quiet place and a quiet moment to do it. God may have more to reveal to you in addition to what He has already given me.

There are some parts of the prayer that are distinguished by sex or relationship status. This is intentional, as the prayers are specific and apply to men and women separately, as well as to couples and singles.

So, I just finished my final readthrough of the book to ensure it is fully formatted...and the Holy Spirit just instructed me to add to the prayer. Specifically, He wants me to deal with incest, shame, pedophilia and even those who were perpetuators.

This may not pertain to everyone, but there is someone He desires to free in this area. To not jar you, I felt it appropriate to warn you before you start the prayer.

*I *YOUR FULL NAME* repent for having sex outside of marriage and attaching myself to those God did not deem my spouse.*

Lord, I also repent for any form of incest that I may have participated in. No matter my age at the time, whether I was the perpetuator or the victim. I also repent for anyone I may have touched inappropriately or even assaulted. I repent and I ask for your mercy. I pray that whatever doors I opened in my life, and in the life of any victims or even in the life of the generation to come be shut because of my repentance. I renounce, denounce and come out of agreement with the spirit of incest, molestation and pedophilia and I declare that my sexuality and the sexuality of my future generations are under the blood of Jesus.

Lord, I also make a conscious decision to forgive anyone in my family who may have abused me in this way. I also extend forgiveness to myself for any wrongdoing that I committed.

I come out of agreement with the spirit of fear and shame. I stand on 2 Timothy 1:7 *"For God has not given us a spirit of fear, but of power and of love and of a sound mind."* **I declare that I am the righteousness of God in Christ Jesus and that He has forgiven me, and that He is pleased with me. Lord, because I fear you and hope in you, I stand on** Psalm 147:11 *"The Lord takes pleasure in those who fear Him, In those who hope in His mercy."*

Lord, I declare today that every torment is broken off of my mind, memories, my soul, my spirit and my emotions. I will no longer listen to the lies of the enemy, but I stand in Your power, Your love, and declare that I have a sound mind.

Father, I break every covenant, contract, marriage, or agreement that I have personally made through my words, actions and sexual acts and close any shared spirit portals. I also tear down any altars that were built in my bloodline, and I divorce any spirit spouses by reason of the authority of the blood of Jesus.

Lord, your word states in I John 1:9 *(NKJV), "If we confess our sins, He is faithful and just to forgive us our sins and to cleanse us from all unrighteousness."* **By reason of** *my sincere confession and repentance, I receive forgiveness and cleansing.*

Your word says, in Matthew 26:28 (NKJV), "For this is My blood of the new covenant, which is shed for many for the remission of sins." Therefore, I apply the blood of Jesus as the new covenant over my life and declare that I receive full remission and that every other covenant is now null and void. I break every covenant, contract or marriage made in my name and made with or without my consent with any man, woman, spirit or the kingdom of darkness in the name of Jesus and close all shared spirit portals.

I take off and destroy all rings, wedding bands, jewelry, veils, or wedding clothes that I may be wearing spiritually in the name of Jesus and sever all physical connections in Jesus' name. I tear up and burn up all contracts, agreements, and covenants connecting me to anyone that God has not ordained as my spouse in Jesus' name.

*I *YOUR FULL NAME* divorce, and break every spirit, soul, heart, mind and emotional connection in Jesus' name. I break every covenant, agreement, or contract made in my name with or without my consent or through my interactions and or sexual relationships* *with* ***LIST FULL NAME OF ALL PAST SEXUAL PARTNERS*.** *I renounce, denounce, and sever all connections, whether mental, spiritual, emotional, physical, relational, or financial, with them and those they may be connected to and close all shared spirit portals in Jesus' name.*

I remove every thought, imprint, scent, desire, memory, or attachment from any and all ungodly relationships in Jesus' name from my heart, mind, soul, spirit, will, emotions, and memory. I plead the blood of Jesus over my heart, my mind, my soul, my spirit, my body, my relationships, my marriage or future marriage, my career, finances, desires, emotions, memories, and all that God has for me or that is connected to me in the name of Jesus.

Lord, I forgive anyone who opened the door to sexual immorality in my life. I forgive and release anyone who hurt me, whether relationally, physically or sexually. I forgive ***THEIR FULL NAME(S)*.** *I release them from my heart, my mind, my soul, my emotions and my spirit. I bless them in the name of the Lord. Your word says in Luke 6:28 28 (ESV) "bless those who curse you, pray for those who abuse you." I choose to forgive them and bless them today.*

Your word declares in II Corinthians 5:17 (NKJV), "Therefore, if anyone is in Christ, he is a new creation; old things have passed away; behold, all things have become new." Therefore, because I am in Christ, I am now a new creation. I plead the blood of Jesus over my hormones. I declare that my oxytocin, vasopressin, and dopamine receive recalibration by the power of the blood of Jesus. I command my hormones to the obedience of Christ and declare that they receive full restoration of their original design.

MEN: *I call my seed back from *NAMES OF ALL PAST SEXUAL PARTNERS* and remove my testosterone, prostaglandins, cortisol, and immune-modulating proteins from their physical bodies and their systems and command them to go where Jesus sends them.*

WOMEN: *I command all testosterone, prostaglandins, cortisol, and immune-modulating proteins out of my physical body and my systems and command them to go where Jesus sends them.*

I decree and declare that every biological and emotional connection and cycle is broken by the power and authority of the blood of Jesus.

I repent for knowingly or unknowingly harming past partners. I ask that the mercy of God covers and removes the repercussions I earned through my actions. I release healing, forgiveness and restoration to all past partners. I close and sever every spiritual, emotional and hormonal connection opened by pornography, fantasies, adultery, guilt, shame, lust, perversion, molestation and/or unforgiveness.

I apply the blood of Jesus over every accusation that is being raised against me in the spirit realm by reason of Colossians 2:13-14 (NKJV) which says, "And you, being dead in your trespasses and the uncircumcision of your flesh, He has made alive together with Him, having forgiven you all trespasses, having wiped out the handwriting of requirements that was against us, which was contrary to us. And He has taken it out of the way, having nailed it to the cross."

I remove myself and bloodline from any altar speaking perversion, lust, molestation, pedophilia and adultery in Jesus' name. Permanently, perpetually, and effective immediately. I repent for my bloodline for the spirit of rebellion, manipulation, witchcraft, and stubbornness, for your word says in I Samuel 15:23a (NKJV) "For rebellion is as the sin of witchcraft, And stubbornness is as iniquity and idolatry..."

I repent for any sin of bloodshed, and I tear down those altars by the blood of Jesus. I ask Jesus that You would drain and dry up any altar of blood and replace it with the pure blood of Jesus Christ. Your word says that the blood of Jesus speaks a better word than the blood of Abel, "But you have come to Mount Zion and to the city of the living God, the heavenly Jerusalem, to an innumerable company of angels, to the general assembly and church of the firstborn who are registered in heaven, to God the Judge of all, to the spirits of just men made perfect, to Jesus the Mediator of the new covenant, and to the blood of sprinkling that speaks better things than that of Abel."- Hebrews 12: 22 – 24. **Jesus, I ask that You would declare mercy in the places where my sins are crying out for judgment in Jesus' name.**

I exempt myself from the cultural spirits that are in ***YOUR NATIONALITY AND CURRENT PLACE OF DWELLING*** *that are influencing me concerning sex and relationships. I remind the spirit realm that I am not of this kingdom. I am in the world, but not of it, according to scripture. As* John 17: (NKJV) **says,** I also declare "They are not of the world, just as I am not of the world." **By reason of the words of Jesus Christ, I enforce my heavenly citizenship.**

I enforce Hebrews 8:10-13, "For this is the covenant that I will make with the house of Israel after those days, says the Lord: I will put My laws in their mind and write them on their hearts; and I will be their God, and they shall be My people. None of them shall teach his neighbor, and none his brother, saying, 'Know the Lord ,' for all shall know Me, from the least of them to the greatest of them. In that He says, "A new covenant," He has made the first obsolete. Now what is becoming obsolete and growing old is ready to vanish away. For I will be merciful to their unrighteousness, and their sins and their lawless deeds I will remember no more."[1]

I declare that any previous covenant is now obsolete and that the covenant with Jesus Christ is now the only one that stands in my life.

SINGLE: *I declare that my sexually connected oxytocin, vasopressin, and dopamine are covenanted to Christ and under His authority until He brings me to my spouse in the covenant of marriage.*

MARRIED: *I declare that my sexually connected oxytocin, vasopressin, and dopamine are covenanted to Christ and my spouse, ***NAME*** only, and that they are under Jesus's authority.*

I give my entire self; mind, body, soul, spirit, emotions and desires to Jesus. I declare that my mind, body, soul, spirit, emotions, memories, scent, essence, hormones, and sexual organs are cleansed by the living water which is Christ and by His blood and are therefore made pure. I surrender all that I am and every part of my physical, emotional, and spiritual life to Jesus Christ. I receive renewal and restoration through by the authority of Jesus Christ. I will never be the same. Amen.

PRAYER FOR MASTURBATION AND PORNOGRAPHY

Father, I thank you for the power that is in the name of Jesus Christ, Your Son. I thank you that by your mercy and His blood, I can find mercy according to Hebrews 4:16 (NLT), **which says,** *"So let us come boldly to the throne of our gracious God. There we will receive his mercy, and we will find grace to help us when we need it most."*

Lord, I recognize that I have broken your law, and in many ways broken myself, but I thank you for the grace that is available in You for my restoration.

Lord, I repent for opening the door to pornography in my life, and even if someone else opened it, I repent because I kept going back. I repent for agreeing with lust and committing adultery through sexual fantasies of your sons and daughters. They did not deserve the violations that occurred in my mind, whether they were aware of them or not.

Lord, I forgive anyone who opened the door to pornography, masturbation and sexual immorality in my life. I forgive *THEIR FULL NAME(S)*. I release them from my heart, my mind, my soul, emotions and my spirit. I bless them in the name of the Lord. Your word says in Luke 6:28 28 (ESV) " bless those who curse you, pray for those who abuse you." I choose to forgive them and bless them today.

Lord, I repent for masturbation and for molesting myself. I understand that my body is the temple of the Holy Spirit as it says in 1 Corinthians 6:19 (NLT), "Don't you realize that your body is the temple of the Holy Spirit, who lives in you and was given to you by God? You do not belong to yourself." I repent for dishonoring your temple.

I also repent for using my finances to purchase pornography or erotic novels. I pray that your mercy remove any curse that I opened over my finances and bring healing in that area.

I thank you because You are the God of restoration and healing. I pray for healing and restoration of any gray matter that has been affected in my physical brain from pornography. I thank you that you are the resurrection and the life and that any areas where I have suffered death, I ask that You please bring resurrection and resuscitation in those areas.

I pray for healing and recalibration of my hormones in connection with sex. I pray that you please rebuild any structures that I have broken down in my systems, mind, body, soul, spirit and hormones. I pray for new routes to be created in my brain. I cast down every thought and desire that is outside of Your will. I declare and come into agreement with II Corinthians 10:5 (NKJV), which says, "casting down arguments and every high thing that exalts itself against the knowledge of God, bringing every thought into captivity to the obedience of Christ."

I pray for the restoration of sensitivity to my sexual organs where I may have lost sensitivity due to masturbation and divine reversal of all desensitized areas in my emotions, mind, and even physical body.

I pray for the healing and removal of muscle memory when it comes to pornography, masturbation, and sex toys. Please change my desires and give me holy desires. I pray for the cleansing and renewal of my memory bank. Please remove every unclean thought and image that I have seen or meditated on.

I repent for giving the enemy access to my imagination. I enforce your word from this day forward over my mind. I stand and declare agreement and submission to Philippians 4:8 (NKJV) **which says,** *"Finally, brethren, whatever things are true, whatever things are noble, whatever things are just, whatever things are pure, whatever things are lovely, whatever things are of good report, if there is any virtue and if there is anything praiseworthy — meditate on these things."* **I decree and declare that You** *alone have access and authority over my imagination for Your will and Your plans.*

I repent for the kind of pornography that I have watched. I repent for watching and masturbating to ***LIST THEM. EX: VIOLENCE, ANIMALS, HOMOSEXUALITY*,** *and I apply the blood of Jesus over any doors of access I have given to those things in my soul, mind, body, and spirit in Jesus' name. Cleanse me, oh Lord, as only You can.*

Lord, I thank You that in spite of the fact that You fully know me, You still fully love me. I stand on Your love. I dwell in Your love and declare according to Your word, in Acts 17:28 (NKJV), which states, "for in Him we live and move and have our being, as also some of your own poets have said, 'For we are also His offspring."

Let all that I do be done in You and for the glory of Your name. Thank You for loving me and calling me Yours. I am Your righteousness in Christ Jesus. I am a new creation in Christ. The old me is dead, and I am made alive in You. In Jesus' mighty name. AMEN.

As you pray these prayers, I pray that God gives you further revelation of things to tackle. He knows you better than you know yourself, and He desires your freedom. You are loved by God.

FINAL EXERCISE

I leave you with this exercise: Create a chart and write the name of everyone you have had a sexual interaction with, even if it was not full intercourse. Next to each name, write down the attributes and personality traits you remember. Ask the Holy Spirit to bring to mind anything or anyone you may have forgotten.

Then, take note of any traits you see manifested in you that you know were not there before. If they do not align with who God created you to be, rebuke them. By the authority of Christ, command them to go where Jesus sends them.

Finally, please keep in mind that the enemy is not just going to defeatedly skip away and no longer harass you in these areas where you have attained freedom. He plans on coming back.

Luke 4:13 NKJV 'Now when the devil had ended every temptation, he departed from Him until an opportune time.'

Satan did not just leave because Jesus defeated him, he went to bid for an opportune time. Please do not be deceived, he is also waiting on you. Waiting for you to get tired, lonely, angry, frustrated and to fall off your post. He just wants a small lapse in judgement for you to fall back into the cycle. So be vigilant.

I Peter 5:8 (NKJV) Be sober, be vigilant; because your adversary the devil walks about like a roaring lion, seeking whom he may devour.

He is coming. So, you need to stay ready, so you do not have to get ready. Be vigilant about your eyes, your ears, your mind and your heart. Do not allow him any access. Do not allow him to deceive you into thinking that you are strong enough to resist. We have already covered that in Chapter 1. Just RUN.

I am excited to hear your testimonies! What did the Lord show you? Maybe He's given you a strategy that I need. Do not keep it to yourself, share it with someone else.

I love you very much, but most importantly, God loves

NOTES

PART 1

1. Dolan, Eric W. *"Soul Ties: Exploring a Popular Belief in Deep Emotional Bonds."* **PsyPost**, 22 Mar. 2025, https://www.psypost.org/soul-ties-exploring-a-popular-belief-in-deep-emotional-bonds/.

2. Gordon, Christine. "What Is a Soul Tie? Here's Everything You Need to Know." *Brides*, 3 Nov. 2025, https://www.brides.com/soul-tie-explained-5498605

CHAPTER 5

3. Kuhn, S., & Gallinat, J. (2014). Brain structure and functional connectivity associated with pornography consumption: The brain on porn.

JAMA Psychiatry, 71(7), 827–834.
https://doi.org/10.1001/jamapsychiatry.2014.9
3

4. Carter, C. S. (1998). Neuroendocrine
   perspectives on social attachment and love.
   Psychoneuroendocrinology, 23(8), 779–818.
   https://doi.org/10.1016/S0306-4530(98)00055-9

5. Lim, M. M., & Young, L. J. (2006).
   Neuropeptidergic regulation of affiliative
   behavior in animals. Hormones and Behavior,
   50(4), 506–517.
   https://doi.org/10.1016/j.yhbeh.2006.06.028

CHAPTER 6:

6. Schjenken, J. E., & Robertson, S. A. (2020).
   Seminal fluid signaling in the female
   reproductive tract: Implications for
   reproductive success and offspring health.
   Frontiers in Immunology,   11,   356.
   https://doi.org/10.3389/fimmu.2020.00356

7. Gallup, G. G., Jr., Burch, R. L., & Platek, S. M.
   (2002). Does semen function as an

antidepressant? Archives of Sexual Behavior, 31(3), 289–293. https://doi.org/10.1023/A:1015205028451

8. Cera, N., Tartaro, A., Di Pierro, E. D., & Di Paolo, F. (2021). How relevant is the systemic oxytocin concentration for human sexual behavior? A systematic review. Sexual Medicine, 9, 100370. https://doi.org/10.1016/j.esxm.2021.100370

9. Taylor, S. E., Saphire-Bernstein, S., & Seeman, T. E. (2010). Are plasma oxytocin in women and plasma vasopressin in men biomarkers of distressed pair-bond relationships? Psychological Science, 21(1), 3–7. https://doi.org/10.1177/0956797609356507

CHAPTER 7

10. Schjenken, J. E., & Robertson, S. A. (2020). Seminal fluid signaling in the female reproductive tract: Implications for reproductive success and offspring health. Frontiers in Immunology, 11, 356. https://doi.org/10.3389/fimmu.2020.00356

CHAPTER 8

11. Taylor, S. E., Saphire-Bernstein, S., & Seeman, T. E. (2010). Are plasma oxytocin in women and plasma vasopressin in men biomarkers of distressed pair-bond relationships? Psychological Science, 21(1), 3–7. https://doi.org/10.1177/0956797609356507

12. Young, L. J., & Insel, T. R. (2004). The neurobiology of pair bonding. Nature Neuroscience, 7(10), 1048–1054. 7. Taylor, S. E., Saphire-Bernstein, S., & Seeman, T. E. (2010). Are plasma oxytocin in women and plasma vasopressin in men biomarkers of distressed pair-bond relationships? Psychological Science, 21(1), 3–7. https://doi.org/10.1177/0956797609356507

BIBLIOGRAPHY

Prokop, P. (2014). Partner satisfaction, as opposed to condom use, predicts symptoms of depression amongst women: A failure to replicate Gallup et al. (2002). Psychological Reports, 115(2), 437–444. https://doi.org/10.2466/21.PR0.115c21z2

Thomas Nelson. (1982). Holy Bible: New King James Version. Thomas Nelson.

Tyndale House Publishers. (2015). Holy Bible: New Living Translation. (Original work published 1996).

Biblica. (2011). Holy Bible: New International Version. Zondervan. (Original work published 1978)

ACKNOWLEDGEMENTS

Thank you to my amazing family and beautiful friends. Thank you for pushing me, supporting me, and keeping me accountable. Monica, thank you for praying over me and releasing the writing grace. You are a prayer warrior indeed. Kelly, this book would not be what it is without you. Thank you for being a phenomenal last-minute editor.

Mrs. Lawrence, aka Marthe, thank you for your nonsensical attitude about what God has enabled me to do. I'm so grateful to have you as a friend and sister. Jen and Festus, thank you for jumping into this crazy journey with us and for continually pushing me and encouraging me to go beyond my comfort zone. Cherline, thank you for almost 30 years of friendship, and for working on the website so I can finish this book.

Finally, thank you to our Truth In Love community. You daily remind and encourage me that God has called and anointed me for this time and this season. I so love and appreciate each and every one of you.

ABOUT AUTHOR

Ludie Benel-Ponce, M.A., is a teacher, author, and spiritual mentor devoted to helping people walk in truth, freedom, and wholeness. She co-founded Truth In Love with her husband, Pastor Luis, and is the founder of The Inside Job Global, a ministry centered on inner healing, deliverance, and transformation from the inside out.

Ludie carries a clear calling to reveal the mysteries of the Kingdom so that blind eyes may see, deaf ears may hear, and lives long bound may begin to walk in freedom. Through prayer, biblical teaching, prophetic insight, and intentional discipleship, she helps individuals confront what has remained hidden, understand the roots of their struggles, and step into alignment with God's design.

Her work bridges faith, emotional healing, and spiritual truth, offering both compassion and clarity to those ready to move forward. Ludie believes freedom is not rushed, healing is not forced, and restoration is always possible when truth is welcomed.

Together, Ludie and her husband serve through mentorship, teaching, and media that strengthen individuals, restore homes, and impact generations. Her prayer is that every reader leaves this book not only informed, but freer, clearer, and confident in what God is continuing to do.

Readers can stay connected through the Truth In Love Podcast and YouTube channel @WithTruthInLove, as well as on Instagram and TikTok @WithTruthInLove and @LudiePonce. For questions, speaking invitations, access to upcoming teachings, and ministry updates, please email info@withtruthinlove.com

Stay Connected

This journey does not end here.

Scan the QR code to continue growing through the Truth In Love Podcast, YouTube teachings, and encouragement on Instagram and TikTok.

For questions and invitations, email info@withtruthinlove.com

@WithTruthInLove | @LudiePonce